W9-DAL-094

MEDEA

Also available by Brendan Kennelly

The Penguin Book of Irish Verse (Penguin, 1970; 2nd edition 1981)
The Boats Are Home (Gallery Press, 1980)
Cromwell (Beaver Row, 1983; Bloodaxe Books, 1987)
Moloney Up and At It (Mercier Press, 1984)
Mary (Aisling Press, 1987)
Landmarks of Irish Drama (Methuen, 1988)
Love of Ireland: Poems from the Irish (Mercier Press, 1989)
A Time for Voices: Selected Poems 1960-1990 (Bloodaxe Books, 1990)
The Book of Judas (Bloodaxe Books, 1991)

EURIPIDES'
MEDEA

A NEW VERSION BY
BRENDAN KENNELLY

GLEN COVE PUBLIC LIBRARY
GLEN COVE AVENUE
GLEN COVE, NEW YORK 11542

BLOODAXE BOOKS

822.914

Copyright © Brendan Kennelly 1988, 1991

ISBN: 1 85224 188 8   hardback edition
        1 85224 189 6   paperback edition

First published 1991 by
Bloodaxe Books Ltd,
P.O. Box 1SN,
Newcastle upon Tyne NE99 1SN.

3 1571 00131 2217

Bloodaxe Books Ltd acknowledges
the financial assistance of Northern Arts.

LEGAL NOTICE

All rights reserved. No part of this book may be
reproduced, stored in a retrieval system, or
transmitted in any form, or by any means, electronic,
mechanical, photocopying, recording or otherwise,
without prior written permission from Bloodaxe Books Ltd.

Requests to publish work from this book
must be sent to Bloodaxe Books Ltd.

Cover reproduction by V & H Reprographics, Newcastle upon Tyne.

Printed in Great Britain by
Bell & Bain Limited, Glasgow, Scotland.

For Susan Curnow
& Ray Yeates

PREFACE

In 1985 I submitted a version of Sophocles' *Antigone* to the Abbey
Theatre in Dublin. The play was produced in 1986 at the
Peacock, to mixed reviews. One evening in the theatre, a member
of the audience, a woman, walked up to me and said, 'You under-
stand women's rage. Do *Medea* next. Many people say the play is
about jealousy. It's not, it's about rage. Do it.' Having said that,
the woman walked away from me. Her words stuck.

This may be as appropriate a moment as any to say that most
of the insights about life and literature I've picked up from people,
rather than from my own attempts to think, have come from
women. And this learning has happened in the most casual ways,
just like that little encounter in the Peacock Theatre. As far as
I'm concerned, women have a way of saying perceptive things that
is very different from men. They talk to me at times as if they'd
been thinking for quite a while about the particular matter that's
puzzling me; then they say whatever they've got to say candidly
and simply and, to my mind, unforgettably. From their tone of
simplicity and candour, I can tell that they're worth listening to,
and worth following. Why are the words of complete strangers so
compelling? Why do they make coherent and lucid what I'd been
clumsily and blindly trying to come to grips within myself? The
old term "women of the streets" has a very special and valuable
meaning for me. Somehow or other, certain women, when they
decide to do so, get to the core of almost any matter touching on
feelings much more precisely, and with an astounding mixture of
sensitivity and something approaching an unemphatic brutality,
than most men are capable of doing, or even seem to wish to do.

Dublin is a city of maliciously wagging tongues. It is also a city
where unsolicited help and illumination can come your way, if
you learn to listen. Stabs in the back are often compensated for by
wise, kind words to your face. The air is a fascinating blend of
poison and good will.

I spent the best part of the summer of 1986 in St Patrick's
Psychiatric Hospital in Dublin. It was, on the whole, a fine sum-
mer although a very fierce storm hit Dublin in August, causing
the river Dodder to overflow and flood many homes in the Balls-
bridge area of the city. I was trying to recover from prolonged
alcoholism and I found myself listening, listening, especially to
women. The women I listened to ranged in age from about seven-

teen to about seventy. Many of them had one thing in common. Rage. Rage mainly against men, Irishmen like myself. As I listened day after day and night after night to these women talking about men I'd never met, but whom I could recognise in myself, I became aware of the fact that a major reason for their rage was because they were more *conscious* than the men they'd lived with, or left, or been jilted or betrayed or beaten up by. Sometimes these women, these "sick" or "mentally unbalanced" or "mad" women, couldn't fully articulate their feelings about men; but when they could their words were often savage and pitiless and precise. Some of them seemed to me to be unutterably hurt. But even more than that, they were conscious of the hopeless gulf between them and the men they described as cocky, self-indulgent, plausible 'masters' of the house and the pub, the club and the bookie's office, the street and the bed. The rage of these women was the rage of people who'd been used and abused over the years by men who quite often didn't even visit them in hospital. This was the rage the woman who'd spoken to me in the Peacock Theatre a few months earlier had been talking about. This was the rage that I tried to present in *Medea*, because that woman had told me I could. My little room in the hospital felt like a cell of rage. I wrote the first draft of the play in less than a month. I was in touch with that electricity which means that a play or poem goes a long way towards writing itself.

In 1983, I'd published *Cromwell*, a long poem about the man whose name still inspires eruptive hatred in Ireland. Early in 1984 I'd begun work on what was to become *The Book of Judas*, an epic poem trying to deal with betrayal and related matters in history and myth as well as in various kinds of human relationships. My mind was preoccupied with what I called Judasanity, the alternative 'Christianity' that is frequently and widely practised in Ireland, but which insists on not recognising itself for what it is. These women in hospital, expressing their rage at betrayal and violence and cruel indifference, entered *The Book of Judas*. And many themes and preoccupations, even obsessions, in *The Book of Judas* spilled into the rage and accusations of *Medea*. Across cultures, across the centuries, feelings, words and images began to fertilise each other. This kind of cross-fertilisation proves and underlines the delusions, the true madness inherent in that purely chronological view of reality beloved of minds that often condemn the kind of "madness" I met in these women in St Patrick's. (Did the bold St Patrick ever realise what he was giving his name to?).

In turning to Euripides' great play, I knew I was meeting a

woman who, among other things, had deceived her father and murdered her brother, to flee with Jason. She gave all, and expected the same. She was magical, lethal, loving, a sorceress, a barbarian, and had a savage truthfulness in her heart. Euripides presents her as an abandoned, betrayed woman bent on revenge; he also brilliantly suggests the twisted consequences of that revenge. Medea is transfigured into an almost superhuman destroyer by her sense of wrong.

The Medea I tried to imagine was a modern woman, also suffering a terrible pain – the pain of consciousness of betrayal by a yuppified Jason, a plausible, ambitious, articulate and gifted opportunist who knows what he wants and how to get it. Medea, as I imagined her, plans to educate Jason in the consciousness of horror; she destroys his world but leaves him intact; and she instructs him very calmly and lucidly in the appalling consequences of this intactness. All his opportunistic genius for getting a grip on things, for exploiting his macroview of circumstances, now becomes the instrument to lacerate and torment his deepening consciousness of deepening loss. Medea, as I see her, inflicts on Jason the ultimate cruelty: she sentences him to life. This play ends with a cool, horrific talk between two people who, in their different ways, must live with themselves. One senses, however, that this is going to be somewhat harder for Jason.

Medea, when produced, got the sorts of responses that showed its ability to stir very differing and contradictory emotions in people. Most women were moved by it; I received many letters which echoed Medea's feelings about Jason. Some women thought the play was a diatribe against women, the work of a woman-hater who didn't recognise his own hate. Many men didn't like it, felt accused by it, thought it unfair, showing 'only one side of the story'. A few men told me they were grateful for it. One man said I was a bitter bitch in disguise. What disguise, I wonder?

It is true that we disguise ourselves in various ways. *Medea* is a play in which disguises are ripped away. When that happens, the reader and the audience will see what they are, or are not prepared, to see; what they choose or dare to see; and having seen it, what they permit themselves to remember. I remember women, their honest, bitter words in a most humane hospital, talk of a bad storm hitting the city outside, and myself imagining a devastating woman in a cell of rage.

I would like to thank Neil Astley for his excellent suggestions concerning the final shape of this text on the page, and for the note opposite.

MEDEA AND JASON

Medea was a sorceress and priestess of Hecate, the niece of Circe, and daughter of Aeetes, king of Colchis (son of Helios, the Sun god). When Jason came to Colchis with the Argonauts in his quest for the Golden Fleece, Hera caused Aphrodite to make Medea fall violently in love with him, and in exchange for a promise of marriage she helped him overcome the trials devised by her father as a condition for winning the Fleece. Realising that Aeetes meant to kill the Argonauts in the night, Medea warned them and led Jason to the Fleece. During their escape her half-brother Apsyrtus was murdered: some sources claim she dismembered him and left the pieces to delay her father's pursuit; others that she tricked him into a meeting with Jason, who killed him.

Jason was a celebrated hero, the son of Aeson, who should have been king of Iolchos after the death of his father Cretheus. But his uncle Pelias usurped the throne, and Jason's mother arranged for him to be raised in safety by the centaur Chiron. When Jason returned to Iolchos to claim his inheritance, Pelias agreed to resign if he would recover the Golden Fleece, the skin of a miraculous winged ram which had rescued his cousins Helle and Phryxus after their father Athamas had been tricked into sacrificing them to the gods: Helle fell from the ram's back and was drowned in the sea, while Phryxus reached Colchis where he sacrificed the ram to Zeus, and was befriended and then killed by King Aeetes, Medea's father, who kept the Golden Fleece.

When Jason and Medea arrived in Iolchos with the Fleece, Medea claimed she could rejuvenate the old by cutting them up and boiling them in a magic potion, and urged the daughters of Pelias to help her make him young again. The daughters obliged, chopping up their father while he was in a drugged sleep, but Medea disappeared once he was in the pot, and with no magic spell to transform him the usurper was turned into stew instead. Jason's people were so outraged by this that the couple were forced to flee to Corinth, where they lived for ten years, until Jason deserted Medea for King Creon's daughter Glauce. Euripides' play *Medea* tells the story of that betrayal and her revenge. After her flight, she married Aegeus, King of Athens, but was banished by him when she tried to poison his long lost son Theseus. She returned to Colchis, where some sources say she was reconciled with Jason. After her death she married Achilles in the Elysian Fields. Jason was later killed when a piece of his ship fell on top of him.

MEDEA

Brendan Kennelly's *Medea* was first performed by the Medea Theatre Company in the Dublin Theatre Festival at the Royal Dublin Society Concert Hall on 8 October 1988. It was revived on 6 July 1989 at the Gate Theatre, Dublin, prior to a tour of England which took in the Purcell Room at London's South Bank Centre. The cast at the first performance was as follows:

NURSE	Stella McCusker
TEACHER	Geoff Golden
CHORUS	Aine Ní Mhuirí
MEDEA	Susan Curnow
CREON, *King of Corinth*	Liam O'Callaghan
JASON	Michael James Ford
AEGEUS, *King of Athens*	Christopher Casson
MESSENGER	Poll Moussoulides
CHILDREN *of Medea*	Brian Hickey
	Dean Clifford
CREON'S GUARDS	Shay Dunphy
	William Cunningham

DIRECTOR	Ray Yeates
ASSISTANT DIRECTOR	John Breen
DESIGNERS	Chisato Yoshimi
	Katrina McKillen
LIGHTING DESIGN	Bernard Griffin
MUSIC COMPOSER	Noel Eccles
MUSIC PERFORMER	Paul Maher
STAGE DIRECTOR	Marie Breen
ADMINISTRATOR	Arthur Duignan
PRESS OFFICER/PRO	Julie Barber
PHOTOGRAPHS	Tom Lawlor

The play is set outside Medea's house in Corinth.

PART ONE

NURSE. Glory to Heaven for home and family:
a man, a woman, children.
Medea left her home
for love of Jason,
seeker of the Golden Fleece.
Why must a man be always seeking something?
Why must a woman seek a man who seeks his special gold?
Seeking! Seeking! That's the curse and glory of our kind.
But what do we find?
Medea did everything for Jason,
left her home and country for him,
cared for him, loved him, reared his children.
But Jason betrayed her, took another woman.
Medea's love is hatred now.
Jason has betrayed
his children by Medea, to sleep
with a woman of royal blood, the daughter
of Creon who is the ruler of our people.
Medea cannot believe
Jason's treachery, his ambitious lechery.
Kings will be strong on thrones
if they are uppermost in bed.
People are ever eager to believe
what randy kings have said.
(Pause.)
My mistress and her children
have been betrayed by Jason,
the celebrated seeker of the Golden Fleece.
Betrayal is the ripest crop in this land.
The more it is slashed, the stronger it grows.

Ever since Medea heard
of Jason's treachery, she has lain prostrate
on the earth itself, a womanbody of grief,
shrinking with ceaseless tears. Her eyes
are riveted on the clay, as if
she knew that nothing lives above the grass.
Her soul is hurt. She will not listen
to the words of friends, as if these words
were the stupid croaking of crows
in the sky that is more meaningless than dust.
Sometimes, however, she shifts her neck,

her beautiful neck.
Talking clearly to herself, in grief,
about her father and her country and her home –
the home she betrayed to come here
with Jason, who left her in complete contempt,
although she'd left her country for him.
Medea – now Medea knows what it means
to leave a land where there is love
for her in people's eyes,
to live in a country where eyes are cold
with neglect, indifference and contempt.
Medea lives among the faces of an arrogant land.
Arrogance is the inspiration of hatred
and – the gods be with us – she has begun
to hate her own children, the very sight of them.
They are sprung of the seed of Jason,
seeker of the Golden Fleece.
The Golden Fleece, indeed!
Can any man or God tell me
what is the Golden Fleece?
The shearings of a sheep, or sly,
alluring threads of gold?
Whatever Jason seeks – Medea hates.
(Pause.)
When I see her prostrate on the earth
I know she is drinking the knowledge of the evil dead,
the fiery strength of poisoned spirits,
the secrets of malignant centuries.
What is growing, this very moment,
in her prostrate mind?
Even as a girl, Medea had a dangerous
way of thinking about herself and others.
She will tolerate no hurt or harm to her heart.
I know Medea. She frightens me.
She is prostrate now, but when she rises from the earth
she may steal into the palace
where Jason lies, drive a sword
into his heart, his belly, chop
his penis and his testicles for the pure pleasure of revenge.
So there lies Jason of the Golden Fleece!
Fleece is what he sought, blood is what he found.
(Pause.)

Among women, Medea has the most cunning mind of all.
She is fox and badger, ferret and stoat,
eagle and hawk.
She can master seven kinds of talk,
using the same words.
She is the clouds the sun cannot penetrate,
she is the sun the clouds cannot resist,
she is the voices of the rain,
she is the silence of an unread book,
she has a tongue to flay anyone who
bandies words with her. Those who
feel the lash of that tongue take
a long time to heal. A few have
never found the cure. The day may come again
when she'll be as fierce and deadly
as she seems broken now.

Enter TEACHER *and* BOYS.

Here come the children
from their play, free of the thoughts
that make their mother prone with hurt
and anger on the earth, as if she cannot
wait to become part of it. Such thoughts
are far from children's playful hearts.

TEACHER. Why are you standing alone at the gate,
muttering to yourself? Where is Medea?
Why are you not with her?

NURSE. Medea's sorrow is so deep,
so driven into the earth, I
had to come out to tell the wind
and sun, to tell the patient, listening sky
itself, the story of her sorrow.

TEACHER. Is Medea still crying?

NURSE. Medea's grief is only starting.
Her tide of bitter sorrow is only
at its source.
                    She is prostrate now.
When she is upright, let Jason be careful.

TEACHER. Medea knows nothing
of what is in store for her.

NURSE. What?

TEACHER. Certain things must not be said.

NURSE. Out with it, old man.
    (*Pause.*)
    Speak, or die accursed.

TEACHER. I walked beside the sacred waters
    where the old men sit and talk
    (in mockery or affection I know not).
    These old men look like scruffy, mocking prophets.
    As I passed, one of them
    laughed aloud,
    saying that Creon,
    ruler of this country,
    planned to expel Medea and her children
    from this clean city
    back to her own stinking land.
    Creon, the old man said, held that
    Medea, a cunning woman,
    and her little brats
    were not worthy to live
    in this fair land he rules.
    Pollution, he said, takes many forms,
    and woman is the worst.
    Her stink is natural and inevitable,
    the hot, strong stink of a roused, prowling cat.
    She uses perfume and powder to conceal it
    but most of all, she uses cunning.
    I am a teacher, I know boys and girls.
    I know that Creon's words are lies
    but I dare not say so in public.

NURSE. Will Jason allow his children
    to be pitched into exile?

TEACHER. Old loves are graves,
    new loves grow out of rotting corpses.
    To Jason, Medea's love is dead,
    a lost excitement buried in the past.

NURSE. Our lives are finished here.
    The shame of exile is the worst of all.
    An exile belongs nowhere, his name is nothing,

16

his memory is scurrilous and impoverished
he is the true outsider because he is outside
himself, the little quiet
familiar things that make his soul.
If Creon sends us into exile,
he puts in exile all our souls.
Exile is the worst form of living death.

TEACHER No sermons on exile, my dear.
Keep quiet. Not another word.
This is no time for Medea to hear your grisly story.

NURSE. (*To the* CHILDREN.)
Do you see what your father is doing to you?
Because your father is my master, I cannot wish
him dead, but he is showing
the most callous hatred
to you, the children of his blood,
who should be one
with the beat of his heart.
This cannot be natural.
Where is your father's love for you?

TEACHER. Do you not realise that people love themselves
more than anyone else in the world?
Is there one person in this city today,
in this house tonight,
who can swear he loves his neighbour
more than himself? That is not to say
love does not exist, shyly, in the hearts
of men and women. And yet, my experience
as a teacher of boys and girls
tells me they love themselves more than others,
rehearsing to become decent men and women,
respectable, house-owning, careful,
somewhat ulcerous perhaps,
threatened with (let's say) angina,
that sweaty tightening of the chest,
that chilling of the hands and feet.
Consider one such man. In a gesture of defiance
against himself and what he stands for,
he becomes, one summer evening, a little tipsy.
There grows in him a strange compulsion

to spill his little, hidden agonies
into the ear of a twitching stranger
who has left his wife and children
for reasons that he tries to drown in a glass,
seeing himself risking a thrilling freedom
in some hallucinating city of the future.
But come, I am frogleaping the centuries.
Still, that is a teacher's privilege –
the one inspiring madness his profession allows –
the knowledge that all things happen at the same time,
to the same people (though they all die)
as the centuries flow by, smiles upon their lips
at the spectacle of honest, helpless repetition.
It is a simple tale. People love themselves
as they sense they should.
Failing in this, they invent a successful god
and plague him with their failures.

NURSE. (*To the* CHILDREN.)
Inside. Inside with you!
(*To the* TEACHER.)
Keep these children as far from Medea
as you possibly can. Don't let them come
within an inch of their mother
especially when that icy anger freezes her eyes
and freezes all within the orbit of her rage.
Because of that rage, people will die.
May it be her enemies that die, not her friends.

MEDEA. (*Within.*) Grief!
I curse this life of grief and pain
heaped on me by the man
that I created with my blood
until he thought he was a god.
His love was life to me.
It is an insult now.

NURSE. (*To the* CHILDREN.)
Dear children of my heart,
your mother's heart
is troubled beyond words, her
anger is a storm in her blood.
So quick, quick, children, hurry indoors

18

as quickly as you can. Above all don't
go near her, don't let her fix
her eyes on you, her kiss
is deadly, her caress
a warm poison. Her touch is
gentle, but her will is iron.
Go on, my children, go indoors,
be quick. Quick.

The CHILDREN *leave with* TEACHER.

(*Pause.*)
                  Soon Medea's
grief will burst over this
world in a never-before-known storm
of rage. Men will have forgotten
the name of peace. Has peace a name?
Will Medea destroy the name of peace
and put a fake word in its place?
Will the real word be destroyed
by Medea's rage? Is this her
rage – to falsify all words, so that
men and women, in their talk,
are capable of nothing but lies?

Is her rage directed against
children learning words, against
the wordless child in the womb? Has
Medea made women the carriers of liars?
And what is Medea, fierce, true,
trusting, self-willed Medea, to do
with men-liars, child-liars,
liars unborn?
                  Will Medea allow
child-liars grow up to be
father-liars who will beget child-liars, who will
become father-liars to beget child-liars? Only
the earth is true, we must shelter
ourselves from it, protect our
valuable lies as we protect our
children, clothe them, teach
them to communicate. Insure them.
Educate them. Bless them. Send them out

into the world to bring new children
to the earth. The world of rage.
Medea's world. The world of rage.
World without lies. Well-dressed lies.
Stylish lies. Legal lies. Family lies.
Religious lies. Politicians' lies.
Writers' lies. Theatre lies.
Actors' lies. Audiences' lies.
Critics' lies. Husbands' lies. Poets' lies.
Judges' lies. Wives' lies. Girls' lies. Teachers' lies.
Doctors' lies. Lovers' lies. Kings' lies.
The lies of writing about lies.
The lies of words. The lie that is
at the heart of all lies –
the truth, and the hot-faced seekers
after truth. The lies of those who
think they have cut the lies out of their hearts,
the lies of hearts who think they are the sole
possessors of the truth.

MEDEA. (*Within.*) Wronged, wronged, I am wronged
in every deepest corner of my being.
My sons, your father hates me
and every day you live is but a curse.
May death sweep your father
and sweep you too, my children,
and sweep away to blackest hell
every trace and sign
of this accursed family.

NURSE. Medea! Why do you bring
curses on your entire household?
Why will you make your sons
suffer for their father's sin? Why
must these innocent boys
bear the scourges of a guilty man?
(*Pause.*)
The souls of many kings and queens
are poisoned, vindictive to the end.
The more stylish their talk,
the more hardened their hearts.
They are made proud and pitiless
by their great reputations.

They are so used to giving commands
they cannot bear the thought of being checked.
This royal cocksureness will scorn all advice
though that advice be born of loving friendship.
It is more civilised
to live among your equals.
Your heart is more at ease.
I have no wish to be a sad old queen
shaking hands with every wide-eyed idiot
at some show or exhibition.
I'd prefer a pleasant, calm old age,
rocking gently with memories.
I pity royalty and its fatal obstinacy,
its fixed and stupid smile into the crushing mob,
its ludicrous elegance among the tatters,
its handsome hypocrisy, its descent
from murder, pillage, rapine, iniquity.
Mortals should practise moderation.
With moderation, old age can be a joy.

Enter CHORUS.

CHORUS. I heard a cry. It was
       a woman's cry, fierce, piercing and demented
       in the grip of some unbearable pain.
       It was Medea's cry – no woman
       ever cried like Medea. It is like
       the cry of Nature itself, the cry of creatures
       losing their young in the wilderness, the cry
       of a woman who knows she has a dead child
       in her womb, the cry of the hare
       when the hound's teeth sink into its neck.
       But Medea's cry was deeper, purer, wilder
       than any of these. It was the cry
       of the first woman
       betrayed by the first man.
       It turned that very house into a cry.
       That house is dear to my heart.
       My heart echoes with Medea's cry.
       She has my pity now, she always will.
       I am loyal to her still.

NURSE. Jason's house was once a home.
       It is a home no more.

The life has left it.
(*Pause.*)
Jason has a mistress in his bed
while Medea wastes away in her room.
Not a word of comfort can come
within a million moon-miles of her heart.

MEDEA. (*Within.*)   I want my brain
to be set on fire by a lightning-bolt from Heaven,
to burn out of my head those eyes
that have witnessed the treachery of men.
Men speak of good. Tell me, o tell me what is good?
Tell me, truly, what is the good of living?
I admit the hatred in my heart
for what I thought was good,
the pride and promise of those golden days.
I wished to live that promise without lies.
A lie is a kind of death. I will not continue
to live in this house of lies.

CHORUS. Medea, you are going mad with sadness,
your body is shrivelling at the thought
of another woman in your man's bed.
But why bother to lust for that particular bed?
Or are you so sick of living
that you cherish the thought of dying?
I pray you, do not pray for that.
Live, my dear Medea, live.
You are strong, imaginative, resourceful.
If your husband loves another woman,
that is a common thing. All over this city
men hurry to their lovers, or wait for them
where their beds are soft and warm,
where love can spend itself like any season,
can shed the guilt that is the enemy of love,
can kill the cold distance that makes
potential lovers strangers to each other.
This city is full of lovers, Medea.
It is also full of strangers.
Be a stranger if you will,
be a lover, if you can.
The man you believe you love is but one man.
Let no one man destroy your life.

This city teems with lovers. Find one.
Love him.

MEDEA. (*Within.*) Dear gods,
I left my father, I killed my brother,
I created my husband.
My husband broke his oath.
The answer is fire
or the sword
or the deadly wandering of poison
in the guise of irresistible beauty.
Beauty, poison, fire,
fire that will be a rival to the sun,
fire that will become a fire of legend
because Jason broke the oath he made to me,
to me, Medea.

NURSE. Medea knows the meaning of prayer.
She knows the meaning of revenge. And she has
schooled her heart in rage beyond my comprehension.

CHORUS. Whatever wisdom I possess is at her service.
Nurse, I beg you bring her here, I beg you
bring her out of that place. Tell her
I am her friend. Hurry, before she wreaks
havoc in the palace. There is no limit
to the fury of such a sorrow, no
boundary to the fierceness of such rage.

NURSE. I'll try, I'll try.
She has a fierce look in her eyes,
especially if she thinks you're going to speak to her.
I think she thinks all human words are lies,
that never again can any word be true.
Her eyes rage: idiots and lunatics –
that's the right name for poets
who make up songs to celebrate
the joy of life at feasts and banquets,
but never have discovered a song or poem
or music to rid the world
of pain and sorrow, all the horrors
that drive men and women to their graves.
Music and poetry are pretty ornaments,
trivial and attractive, but mere distractions

from the wormy rot that waits us all.
(*Pause.*)
I'll try to fetch Medea now.

NURSE *goes in.*

CHORUS. I hear a woman's cry of grief.
      She cries of misery, of bad luck,
      of the horrors of marriage, of broken
      oaths, of love betrayed.
      Every sound she utters is such
      a cry of grief, all language could be
      drowned in it. She makes me think that
      the saddest words are only a failure to cry.

Enter MEDEA.

MEDEA.
      (*To audience, looking also from time to time at the* CHORUS.)
      Women of this city,
      do not turn critical eyes on me.
      I have come out of that place.
      Your eyes are full of judgement
      but devoid of justice.
      He's a snob! She's a whore! He's a drunkard!
      I pitch judgement to the winds
      and cry for justice.
      I cry for justice though my life is over.
      It is the sweet taste of life I have lost,
      I who have tasted the sweetest moments life can offer,
      so sweet I knew they could not last.
      Sweetness is brief, bitterness is long.
      The man who was my world, my sun and moon and stars,
      my sacred rivers and holy mountains,
      has proved himself not a man, but a poisonous snake.
      And yet he feels and thinks,
      schemes, manipulates and plans,
      handles emotions as if they were money
      which he deposits safely in his pocket,
      fingering them for comfort or for fun.
      O yes, he feels and thinks.
      And yet, of all the creatures
      the fertile mind of Nature has conceived
      there are no creatures who can

feel and think like women. That is why
we are the unhappiest creatures
on the face of this creative earth.
First, all dressed in white, for the most part,
we are the playthings of men's bodies,
the sensual toys of tyrants.
Men, the horny despots of our bodies,
sucking, fucking, licking, chewing, farting into our skin,
sitting on our faces, fingering our arses,
exploring our cunts, widening our thighs,
drawing the milk that gave the bastards life.
And allowing for all that, there's another problem –
is he a good man or a bad?
Till the day he marries,
a man can conceal his true nature
by the careful exercise of style.
Style – that elegant lie.
After marriage, his true nature begins to emerge.
Marriage, happy, horrible, or dull, is revelation.
If separation follows, the woman
is often the object of sniggers,
the man, an object of sympathy.
If the marriage remains intact,
a woman needs second sight in order
to handle this stranger who is her
bedmate. What are his expectations,
his midnight tricks, his desires
to hurt or be hurt, his
terrified or savage ways, his
cold kindness, his savage
caresses, his lawful barbarisms,
the tragedy and comedy of
intercourse, his sudden loss of
interest in her body, his
turning his back on her as if
she didn't exist (does she? my friends)?
Does a woman really exist
apart from the "attention" a man
pays to her? Usually, this
"attention" happens in the warm
creaking of the bed, the rhythm
that leads to snores on one

side, and, often enough, tears
on the other. Tears and snores.
Silence and noise. Woman and man.
(*Pause.*)
It is often said that
we women have a comfortable life
in the safety of our homes, while
men go out to sweat at work,
or risk their lives in the terrible
dangers of war. Nonsense.
I'd rather sweat it out
in some stinking hellhole, or
fight a war in a foreign land
than give birth to a brat
who will add to the pollution
of this befouled earth
where even the seas are thick
with poison. However,
women of this city, you and I
are not in the same
position. This is your city.
You belong here.
You are here. Your friends are here.
You are comforted by familiar sights.
I, on the other
hand, am homeless, husbandless,
exiled and forsaken, wronged
by the man I loved, with
nobody to turn to in this
hour of cursed misfortune. Now,
dear sisters, dear women
with whom I have shared
my nightmare, there is one
thing I must ask of you.

If any punishment
falls on my husband's head, if he is
driven naked and lunatic
through the streets, screaming
obscenities most citizens
have never heard before
or even dreamed could

ever exist; if he should
lose what is nearest and
dearest to him in the world,
and storm demented
at the sight or thought
of unbearable loss,
tearing the flesh from
his own bones; then,
my sisters, I ask of you
only one thing: your silence.
Silence, the most powerful
weapon of all. We
women are known and proven
to be gentle, warm, considerate
creatures. But if there is
something terrible to be
done, a woman's
gentleness becomes the most
murderous weapon of all.
and it is all the more murderous
when the silence of women
surrounds the deed. That is why
I ask you all, here
and now, for the gift of your
silence. When I take revenge on Jason
let your silence be my strong approving witness.

CHORUS. Do as you will, Medea,
    for your revenge is just,
    your rage the cry for justice in your blood.
    It is no wonder
    that your blood cries out against injustice.
    It is no wonder
    that you would reduce your husband
    and the woman in his bed
    to ashes, and fling these ashes
    wherever the winds may carry them.
    But wait! Here comes Creon,
    ruler of our land,
    bristling with new plans.
    Prepare to listen to a man.

Enter CREON.

CREON. I'm afraid of you.
> You are a woman schooled in evil.
> I am a man who senses evil, and is afraid of it.
> You are maddened by the loss of your man's love.
> Your eyes are burning pools of madness.
> Evil seeps from every pore of your body.
> I know about your threats to kill
> bride, bridegroom and father of the bride.
> Therefore, before you harm me and my kind,
> I will harm you and yours.
> You are to be driven into exile from my land,
> You and your two sons. This exile will take place today.
> Now. Without a single moment of delay. Without a word.
> Get out of this land.

MEDEA. I am not an evil woman. I am a skilful woman.
> Because I am skilful, I make distinctions.
> Because I make distinctions, some people hate and fear me.
> You say you are afraid of me.
> Creon, my King and master, you have no need to fear me.
> Fear the power of rumour, the envious blood,
> the malignant energy of wagging tongues.
> I was not born to harm great kings.
> I hate my husband.
> You have done no wrong against me,
> yet you are afraid you will suffer
> harm at my hands.
> Why, in the name of all the gods, should I harm you?
> You have exercised a father's right –
> You have given your daughter
> to the man you consider worthy.
> That is natural, dignified, and proper.
> How could I hate a man of such integrity?
> Never.
> It is my husband I hate.
> (*Pause.*)
> You are a wise king.
> May the gods bless
> every moment of your future,
> but allow me and my two sons
> to live in the shadow of the goodness of your rule.
> If there is evil in me, it will be

driven into exile by your goodness and wisdom.
I have been foully used, but under you,
my King and master, that foulness will be dispelled,
and be replaced by good.

CREON. No! I cannot afford to listen to you.
You have a tongue to make
almost any man change his mind,
but not Creon's mind, not the mind
of the King of the people.
Though there is praise and comfort in your words,
they do not lessen the fear in my heart.
In fact, I trust you now even less
than when we began to speak.
Your persuasiveness has increased my fear.
(*Pause.*)
It is easier for a man to defend himself
against a hot-tempered woman
than against a woman with an icy mind
and a cool tongue. The most difficult
obstacle of all is a woman's silence –
it makes a man feel that his words are less
than the squeaking of mice in the sleeping dark.
So leave me now, and no more words.
My mind is made up. Go, no more words.
Your words of praise will turn
to hate of me. I cannot listen.
I *must* not listen. At this moment,
I wish the gods would make me deaf.
(*Pause.*)

MEDEA. Most royal and just of kings,
I beseech you by your loving eyes
on the young bride...

CREON. Your words are falling on deaf ears.
You will never move me from my resolution.
I will not be convinced by the words
of a woman who has admitted
hatred for her husband.

MEDEA. It is the truth. You are
a known lover of the truth.

CREON. (*Pause.*) I love my family
more than I love the truth.

MEDEA. The loves of men are sometimes a great evil.

CREON. Get out of my way, woman.
Trouble me no more.

MEDEA. My troubles are my own.
My life is a list of troubles.

CREON. Throw her out.

MEDEA. No, not to be thrown out by servants.
I beg you, Creon –

CREON. Don't beg. Go.

MEDEA. I am ready to go.

CREON. Then why are you clutching me
so fiercely, as if you would
never let me go, as if you would
move me from my place?

MEDEA. I don't care
about myself, but I ask you to take
pity on the children. Creon, you
yourself are the kind father
of a princess. Kindness to children
is natural, the very sweetness
of the heart. Let me stay here
for one day to get myself and my children
ready for exile. Their father doesn't care,
so all the responsibility for our departure
falls on my shoulders.
I don't care about myself. It's
for my children I am crying now.
Mercy, Creon. Mercy for one day,
one last, loving, caring, crying day.

CREON. I know that I am making a mistake.
But let me give you one warning,
and one warning only.
If, when the sun rises tomorrow,
you and your children are found
within the boundaries of this land,

the three of you will die in that instant,
on that very spot.
You say I love the truth.
I have never spoken a truer word.
You may stay here for one day.
One day is not enough for you to do
what fills my heart and soul
with fear. One day, Medea, one day:
Do your work, then go your way.

Exit CREON.

CHORUS. Wretched Medea! Where will you go now?
Is there, somewhere, a kindly
stranger to take you in? Or
will you become a muttering
wanderer through unknown lands,
a tattered, hungry beggar
among strangers, at home in
the dirt of the world, ignored
by all but those with pity or
contempt in their eyes? Nothing
faces you but trouble. Trouble is
your husband now.

MEDEA. Trouble? Nothing faces me but trouble?
There's trouble ahead for the bride and groom,
there's trouble ahead for Creon.
Do you think I'd ever have spoken to the King just now
if I were not sure of my own plans?
If I were not sure of what I am going to do
I would not have spoken to that fool
nor clutched him, as he said, 'fiercely'.
Men love to be held 'fiercely',
it makes them think a woman weak.
But Creon is such a fool,
Such a victim of his own soft mercy,
that though he might have spoiled my plans
by shaming me into exile,
he has allowed me one day,
one sweet, vicious, vengeful, devastating day,
to make three corpses –
one of Creon, man of mercy,

one of his daughter, thief of my man,
one of my man, snake of my bed.
He will be a living corpse.
My sisters, I can think
of many ways of ridding the world of these three.
Fire appeals to me.
So does the sword.
Yet I believe I shall choose
the method for which I am most fitted.
Poison. Poison spreads slowly, unstoppably,
like the coming of a sick old age.
Think of poison spreading through
the bodies of lovers in the bridal bed.
The sort of poison I will inflict
will be deep and slow and constant
as the suffering I have endured.
There is nothing unfair in that.
Justice is granite.
All these days and nights when I cried and cried
something in me said
Justice will not be denied.
So, let me
imagine them dead. What city,
knowing the crime, would offer me
protection? Where can I be safe?
I must wait to carry out
the murders in secrecy. However,
if necessary, I shall do it
by the sword, and die, of course.
I don't fear that.

This is hard work. Hard work –
the source of all true happiness.
Never before
did I feel the fullness of womanhood,
the danger emanating with every breath.
It is exhilarating, irrepressible, new,
as though I were an army in myself.
Gentleness, timidity, have buried my ferocity.
What men call "charm" has quelled my real talent.

Betrayal has proved to me the evil of good men's consolation.
I am at home in my own evil.

It is the only force that brings justice
into this perfumed, jewelled, stylish world
of absolute injustice. A little poison,
properly administered, may restore the hope
of that lost justice that compelled us
to give respect to others, and dignity
to the mind of man. A little poison
may perform the miracle.

CHORUS. The rivers of the world
    have turned round, flown against themselves
    to find their origins. They defy the laws
    that make them flow naturally to the sea.
    The earth, and the moral laws that
    help to keep the world beautiful
    and fertile, have entered a most
    destructive madness. Treachery
    and betrayal have gripped the hearts
    of men, so that they sneer
    at Heaven's laws. But there will
    come a change, the voice of
    Heaven will be heard, and
    the true glory of women will
    enrich the centuries, kind wisdom
    echoing down the ages as
    the unpolluted river sings itself
    forward in joyous fluency
    to the sea. With equal joyous fluency,
    the time is coming when honour
    will be paid to women, when
    their feelings will not be made
    by men, when slavery will not
    masquerade as love, when
    a man's tone of voice will not
    create a tremor in a woman's
    reply, when a woman will
    not live to please
    an inferior man, when a woman
    will not sit in silence while
    her master broods in sullen
    superiority, when decisions
    are her agreement to his

suggestions, when her hate
can show itself, articulate
and pure. Then, too, the
shadow of justice may be
thrown across the earth,
like a warm coat across
the shoulders of a shivering beggar.

There will be songs
to celebrate the terrible truth
of women. There will be
womansongs in answer to the false
songs of men.

You, Medea, you
woman among women,
left your father's home
to live in a foreign land.
Tonight, your bed is empty, your
lover a bitter memory, you are
a wretched woman, nothing faces you
but exile. Yet, Medea,
you are a true woman, one
who is not "civilised" by men,
a woman not moulded
by weaklings who are so afraid
of women they must show
their superiority, their indolent
or furious strength, their
"manhood". "Manhood."

A hood worn over
the head of a man so that he
cannot see, so that he
can be wilfully blind.
Pity the man who does not question his manhood.
Manhood is not instinctive strength.
Manhood is deliberate blindness.

Deliberate blindness
will not be true to oaths. Deliberate
blindness has nothing but contempt
for honour. Honour is outraged

and has taken refuge in the clouds. Medea,
you know where you stand.
Woman among women, you cannot
return to your father's house, you
are alone, and another woman,
a princess, has stolen
your husband, shares his bed,
and taken your place. That is
who you are, Medea, in this world of men.

Enter JASON.

JASON. I have frequently observed
that an intractable woman
is impossible to handle.
She is incapable of listening to reason
and resorts to loud, incessant cursing
as though she were unaware
of the infinite possibilities of that civilised language
which has taken centuries to render
logical and lucid.
When you might have held your tongue
and spoken in a fit way to your superiors,
your words were barbarous and arrogant.
Your savage language has guaranteed your exile.
Had you exercised discretion you would be safe.
The only mastery you have is of abuse.
Not that your abuse troubles *me* in the slightest.
Continue saying that Jason is the basest of men.
But as for your abuse of royalty, know
you are lucky that exile is
your only punishment. I spent a lot
of time persuading Creon to allow
you to stay in this land. But,
obstinate woman, you simply kept on
abusing the king. That is why
your vile and poisoned tongue will send you into exile.
You'd have been a happy woman
if you'd been born without a tongue in your head.
In spite of that, I have come here
to offer money to you and the children.
Exile is hard, and very expensive.
I know you hate me with all your heart.

I cannot think of you with cruelty.
Please accept my offer of money
and of whatever help you need.
I will give you what I can.
(*Pause.*)

MEDEA. Stink of the grave, rot of a corpse's flesh,
    slime of this putrid world,
    unburied carcase of a dog in the street,
    the black–yellow–greeny spit of a drunk at midnight –
    these are my words for you.

    You dare to come to me, my worst enemy.
    You know this is not bravery,
    not generosity,
    but the triumphant ugliness
    on the face of a traitor,
    the offer of money that stresses
    what you think is your mastery,
    your marriage with royalty.
    But I am grateful for your coming.
    It will comfort me to speak of your betrayal
    and it will hurt you more to hear it.

    I won the Golden Fleece
    for you. Then, forsaking my home
    and my loved ones, I followed you,
    deepening in love, diminishing in wisdom.
    Every danger you faced, I met and overcame.
    I was your fighting spirit,
    I was your sword,
    but *you* accepted the glory.

    And now, though I
    have borne you children, you,
    snake among men, have betrayed me
    and arranged a new marriage.
    Again I say I have borne you children.
    If we had no children, I could
    have understood why you decided
    to marry again. A fresh love
    for a new wife – this I
    could have grasped. But what of
    the pledges we made to each other?

You perplex my heart and mind.
Do you believe that the gods
of the old moralities are dead?
Do you believe that men and women
are now living under a new heartless, mindless morality?
Unhappiness is the wilful forsaking of the proven ways.
An oath is an oath.
Break an oath and the agile demons
of unhappiness leap through your
eyes and mind
and consume your soul.
Demons quarrel and bicker about the tasteful quality
of the soul. Some are bloated,
some shrivel and pine. Some die.
A dying demon is a piteous sight.
(*Pause.*)
A lost woman is a problem.
Jason, answer me this.
Where am I to turn?
Shall I go back to my father?

I betrayed my home and country.
I have nowhere to go.
I have made enemies everywhere
to add to your glory.
A woman kills or charms
that a man thrive and prosper.
What a faithful husband I have in you!
To prove it, I must be driven into exile,
deprived of friends, alone with my two sons.
At the wedding-feast
where stories flow like wine,
don't forget to tell the story
of two children and
a woman who once saved
your life and who are now, all three,
wandering in sluggish beggary.
O gods, why have you
taught us to distinguish gold
from tinsel, yet never
told us how to look at
men's thick bodies so that we

may tell the decent from
the rotten heart?

CHORUS. What does Jason know of Medea's rage?

JASON. It seems I need some skill in speech
to escape the roaring storm of your words.
You have told me what you think.
Let me tell you what *I* think.
It was the Goddess of Love herself
who saved me from the dangers of my quest.
You are a woman gifted
with eloquence and wit
and yet you're but an instrument
in the hands of the Goddess of Love.
It was the Goddess who enabled you
to save my life. Yes, you helped me,
but as I shall now demonstrate to you,
in logical fashion,
you gained much more than you lost.

First you quit a savage land
to live in this dear place where you have come to know
the subtleties of Law and Justice,
rather than the crude ignorance of strength.
Here, men appreciate your wisdom,
you have grown famous in their hearts and minds.
If you were living on some remote island
nobody of consequence would know your name.
May I never have a mite of gold in my house,
may I be denied the gift to sing
a sweeter song than Orpheus,
if my good fortune is to be hidden from men's eyes.
Men have the right to see
and to rejoice in what I've done.
They have the right to know the famous name of Jason.
That is all I have to say
about my finding of the Golden Fleece.
(After all, it was you who started this debate.)
(*Pause.*)
Next, there is the matter of
my marriage with the Princess.
What sane man is not attracted to royal blood?

In this particular matter, which I
consider wise, inevitable and just,
I shall demonstrate three indisputable things:
first, my instinctive wisdom;
second, the sanity and rightness of my choice;
third, the noble service I have
rendered to you and to my sons.
(Please, please hold your tongue
a moment. Have the courtesy
to give me time to speak.)
(*Pause.*)
When I came to this land,
a total stranger in an alien culture,
carrying on my back a load of troubles
my mind festering with painful problems,
what better luck or sweet good fortune
could I, a miserable exile, have
than marry with the King's daughter?
It was not that I was weary of your beauty
(that is the thought that cuts you to the quick
and puts the lightening-madness in your eyes)
or that I was crazy with desire for a young wife;
still less that I wanted to be the father
of many children. The children I have
are enough for me, I have no complaint
or criticism to make of them. No!
what I desired was a comfortable home
where we would always have enough
(for I know well a poor man has no friends
while money binds us together in firm friendship);
and so I wanted to see my children reared
in a manner worthy of their father
and his house. I wanted with all my heart
to give them a proper style
and, fathering other children
to be brothers to the children of your womb,
bring them all together
under one harmonious roof
in health and wealth and happiness.
It was a dream, Medea,
my dream of happiness.

Why should you want more children?
As for myself, it will reward me
to help the children I already have
by means of the children of my new marriage.
Surely that is no evil scheme?
I know you would agree
if jealousy were not binding you.
Why are you so blind, Medea, so tragically blind?

I know that you
women believe that to be lucky
in love is to be lucky in
all things, but if some curse
or sad misfortune hits that love,
you will consider this reasonably decent world
a vile, detestable place.
The world does not change
because of one woman's change of heart.
The gods, in their divine imagination,
should have devised a different way
for men to gather children.
Why should men depend on women to give them children?
Women should not exist.
That way, there would be no trouble in the world.

CHORUS. Jason, you arrange your arguments with plausible skill.
    And yet you have betrayed your wife.
    There is no arguing with that.

MEDEA. Yes! I have many beliefs
    that are not shared by many people.
    I believe, for example, that
    the plausible traitor is the worst kind of scoundrel.
    Plausibility smothers the soul with oily words.
    By comparison, a passionately meant
    insult is a kind of compliment,
    a sort of spiritual bomb to shatter lethargy.
    The plausible man, confident in his
    ability to convince you of his evil
    with fine words symmetrically arranged,
    shrinks from no evil persuasion, because
    evil persuasion is his purpose and his mission.
    And how elegantly he would accomplish it.

There are those who envy him his style.
I have noted that this city is replete
with such men of style, and furthermore,
and sadder still, young men who wish
to imitate the plausible, successful men.
Every plausible man is clever
but it is a limited cleverness.
One burning word of honesty
is enough to reveal its emptiness.
If you were a man,
I mean a man of ordinary honour,
you would have told me about your
intended marriage to the Princess,
not kept it a secret from your sons and me.

JASON. And if I'd told you, I'm sure
you'd have been ablaze with enthusiasm.
Even now, you can't conceal the hate
and resentment in your eyes.

MEDEA. No, my plausible man. You
knew I was ageing, and this
would do nothing to advance your plans.
I had outlived my usefulness.

JASON. I say again, it was not for the sake
of a woman that I enter marriage.
I wanted you to live here in safety.
I wanted to father princes
to be brothers to my sons.
I wanted royalty to spread through my family.
I wanted to distance myself
from poverty and want and shame.
I wanted to kill all possible indignity.
I wanted to establish, forever, a noble family.
Glory to heaven for such a family.

MEDEA. May that family never be mine.
I want no happiness that hurts my soul.
I want the happiness that comes
from *my* husband and *my* children,
mine alone.

JASON. Will you change your
       prayer to the gods, to find better
       sense in yourself? Say – 'May I
       never see a useful opportunity as being
       shameful; may I consider
       no good fortune as being ill.'
       The best prayer is the prayer
       that helps us to cope
       with the folly and evil of this world.
       Pray to make sense of the swirling world.

MEDEA. Your prayer for sense –
       the commonest of common sense –
       is an insult.
                    Prayer is not
       a way of coping with fools.
       Prayer is for dealing
       with the injustice *caused* by fools,
       rhetorical idiots
       and blind, ambitious,
       power-hungry cretins.
       Prayer, my plausible friend, is
       anger at what is, and a longing
       for what should be.
       Prayer is a bomb at the door of your house.
       Being a man of sense,
       you have a palace of refuge.
       Living my passion,
       I am faced with exile.

JASON. You make your own exile.

MEDEA. But what was my crime? Did I
       betray you and marry another
       man so that I could be
       the mother of a Royal Family?

JASON. You cursed the King.
       You heaped curses on the head
       of the ruler of this land.
       You met his hospitality
       with your obscene ingratitude.

MEDEA. On you, and on your house,
    I shall heap such curses
    you'll wish you'd never lived.
    The only blessing you will ever know
    will be your death. That's the blessing
    you will pray for.

JASON. Listen, woman, listen carefully.
    I have no wish to continue this absurd conversation.
    If you wish me to help you
    and my children in your exile, please
    mention it to me. I'm prepared
    to give all the help I can
    with all the generosity in my heart.
    I'm prepared to send letters of introduction
    to all my powerful foreign friends
    who will see to it that you are treated well.
    I have a certain influence
    which I'm prepared to use on your behalf.
    You will not regret it, I assure you.
    If you reject this offer, woman,
    you are both foolish and mad.

MEDEA. Your friends mean nothing to me.
    I will not use those I do not know.
    For the life of me, I cannot accept
    anything from you.
    Do not offer me anything of yours.
    The gifts of men like are plagues.
    They spread contagion among those who touch them.
    You are the poison of my life, Jason, the poison of my life.

JASON. Again, I say again
    that I am willing to help you
    and my two sons in every way.
    You do not know
    what is good for you and for them.
    Think of the children, woman.
    Think of their future.
    If you think of others
    your anger will weaken, then disappear.
    But you are obstinate,
    hugging your anger to your breast

like a favourite child.
Your obstinacy and anger
will cut you off from all your friends.
You will suffer more and more.

MEDEA. Get out of my sight.
There's a young wife waiting for you.
Enjoy her.
One day, perhaps, you will beg
the gods to unmake what seems
the happiness of this fresh union.
So many happy, radiant ceremonies
end in evil.
So out of my sight, plausible man.
Enjoy your new wife, while you can.
(*Pause.*)

Exit JASON.

If the bad strain in a man's love
that once seemed wholesome and true
poisons a woman,
what is she to do?
Should she surrender to that poison,
allow it to spread through her days and nights
until she's dead and forgotten?
Should she pretend, as many women do who want a lover,
the poison does not exist, and so
let it spread, fester and grow
within her till it rots her soul
and all she can do is smile, smile
in poisoned helplessness
at her poisoner and his like?
Let other women live and die as they will,
conquer or surrender according to their style,
let their hearts be poisoned
till they stink of servile hell,
I will not be poisoned by Jason
or by any man.
My heart is strong with that conviction
and I will show it.
If there's poisoning to be done
I will do it.

The time has come
to turn Jason's world upside down
and inside out.
The time has come
for me to act my grief
and for Jason to discover
that in certain unsuspected ways
death may be a matter of relief
from a woman's annihilating pride
when she knows, at last, that she's been cast aside.
Thrown out like an old rag, I know what's true.
I have a single day to do what I must do.
I shall accomplish more in that one day
than Jason in his lifetime; Jason, home-loving Jason,
who told me how to pray.

PART TWO

CHORUS. Love knows no limits
    and may involve man in dishonour,
    shame, drugs, drunkenness, street-wandering,
    confronting strangers, sleeping
    in rainy doorways, even death.
    But if the love is wisely, precisely
    measured, there is no richer
    blessing.

    Therefore, I pray. O goddess, never let
    mad passion consume my heart
    but honour me with the gift
    of moderation. Moderation is
    heaven's fairest gift,
    the very sanity of the gods, their
    sense of fair play at its sweetest
    and most honourable. Moderation keeps
    the demons of excess at bay,
    and makes us grateful for the gift
    of limits.

    To live within limits is to
    honour the infinite, mysterious
    potential of excess. To live by rule
    is to respect every rule-breaking passion
    of which the heart is capable.
    No remorse, no recriminations, no
    vicious, angry quarrels – but I want
    no sluggishness, deadness or
    lethargy either. I want moderation.
    I want the lively consciousness
    of denying myself. I'm not speaking of tameness
    or timidity, I'm speaking of conscious
    moderation.
            O gods, never
    may I be without my city.
    I would rather die than be
    without this city.
    There is no sorrow like that
    of shameful exile. You have
    no friend to turn to in your sickness,
    no affection in the eyes
    of people in the streets.

May the gods
protect me from the man who
would drive me from my city
and its affections. I fear that man
because I love my home.
My truest home is moderation – it's
like living in a house of courage.

Enter AEGEUS, *in traveller's dress.*

AEGEUS. Medea, may the gods grant you
the best of health.

MEDEA.   And to you, Aegeus.
Where are you coming from?

AEGEUS. I've just left the ancient oracle of Phoebus.

MEDEA. Why did you go to the oracle?

AEGEUS. I wanted to know how I might get children.
I wanted to be a fertile man.

MEDEA. And at this stage of your life
are you still childless?

AEGEUS. It seems to be the gods' will that
I am still without a child.

MEDEA. Are you married?

AEGEUS. Yes. Every night we sleep together.

MEDEA. Tell me, Aegeus, what did Phoebus
have to say about children?

AEGEUS. His words were too strange and twisted for me
to understand.

MEDEA. May I ask the god's reply?

AEGEUS.   It takes
a cunning mind to grasp these words.

MEDEA. Tell me, then, what was the oracle?

AEGEUS. I was advised not to let my best wine flow until –

MEDEA. Until?

AEGEUS. Until I return in safety to my home.

MEDEA. Then why do you come here?

AEGEUS. There is a king, the King of Troezen...

MEDEA. A holy man.

AEGEUS. To him, I will reveal the oracle of the god.

MEDEA. He knows a great deal about such matters.

AEGEUS. Yes, and of all the men at whose side
I fought, he is the one I loved most.

MEDEA. I wish you the best of luck, and may
you gain what your heart desires.

AEGEUS. Medea, why are your eyes so sad?
Where is the true beauty of your face?

MEDEA. Jason is wronging me. I never wronged him.

AEGEUS. What has Jason done? Speak plainly.

MEDEA. He has another wife who shares his bed
and shows her power over me, the mother
of his sons.

AEGEUS. Has he done such a shameful, such
a tormenting thing?

MEDEA.   He loved me once.
Now he casts me aside.

AEGEUS. Is he in love? Does he hate your touches?

MEDEA. Yes, this is his grand passion. Nothing else
matters to him.

AEGEUS. Forget him, then, since he has betrayed
his wife and children.

MEDEA. He wants a king for a father-in-law.
He wants power, royalty, and young love in his bed.

AEGEUS. Who gave him the bride?

MEDEA. Creon, the ruler of this country.
(*Pause.*)
My life is in shreds.
(*Pause.*)
Creon is driving me into exile.

AEGEUS. How does Jason allow this?

MEDEA. I beg of you,
Aegeus, to show pity for my misery.
Do not stand apart and see me
driven, helpless and alone, into exile.
Receive me as a guest into
your own country.

I shall pray the gods
to send you the children that
your heart desires.

The path you took to me
was a path of pure good luck.
I shall end your state
of childlessness. I shall help you
create wholesome heirs of your blood.

AEGEUS. With that promise, you have rescued me from madness.
But let me tell you exactly where I stand.
If you yourself come to Athens, I shall
protect you in every possible way.
But I must give you this warning: I shall
not agree to take you with me out of this
city of Corinth. If you yourself come
to my palace, you will find a perfect
refuge and a home. I shall
never surrender you to any man.
But you must escape from this city
through your own efforts.
I'll not be accused
of treachery by my host.

MEDEA. You will not be accused of treachery.
Let me have your oath.

AEGEUS. Do you not trust me?

MEDEA. Yes. I trust you. But in this city
I have powerful enemies, eager
to destroy me. If you were bound
by oath, you would never hand me
over to my enemies, if they tried
to extradite me. But a friendly

agreement of mere words, unstrengthened
by any sacred written pledge,
could easily be melted by shrewd
diplomatic tongues that could persuade you
to become their friend. I have
no power, whereas my enemies
live in the splendour
and power of palaces. That is why
I need your oath.

AEGEUS. You are wise, you are foreseeing.
I will do your bidding.
Dictate the oath.

MEDEA. Swear by the Earth, the Sun
my father's father, by all
the gods, by all –

AEGEUS.   To do what?

MEDEA. Never to expel me from your country,
and never to surrender me
willingly, to any of my enemies.

AEGEUS. I swear by the Earth, by the sacred
splendour of the Sun, by the entire
family of gods, to be true
to the oath that you propose.

MEDEA. And if you break that oath,
what punishment do you pray
to receive?

AEGEUS. The eternal doom of sacrilegious men.

MEDEA. I shall come to your city when I have done
what I intend to do.

Good luck and joy be with you on your journey.

CHORUS (*As* AEGEUS *departs.*)
May the Protector of travellers bring you safe.
May you be the father
of gifted and beautiful children.

MEDEA. O God of justice, magnanimous light of the Sun!
The time has come, my friends, my sisters,

when I shall sing victory-songs
over the bodies of my enemies.
Now I know my enemies will pay the penalty.
Just when all my plans seemed lost and scattered,
Aegeus appeared from another country where,
my work being done, I can live in safety.

Now, my sisters and my friends, let me tell you of my plans.
I shall ask Jason, through a servant, to visit me.
When he comes, he will find every word of mine submissive.
I shall tell him, with all the sincerity
at my command, that I am happy at his royal marriage,
that I have decided it is the best of all good things.
I shall ask him only to permit my children to stay here.
Not that I shall leave them in a land,
a bristling hostile place, for my enemies to insult.
I shall send my sons with gifts for the bride
that she may feel disposed to leave my children in this place.
A handsome robe and a head-dress of beaten gold.
If she puts on the robe, she will die in agony.
Not only she, but anyone who touches her.
Such is the invisible poison in which I steep my gifts.
What I must do next fills me with horror.

I must murder my two sons.
(*Pause.*)
When I have destroyed the house
of Jason, poisoned his princess
and murdered my sons, I'll quit
this land of curses.
No man alive will take my sons from me.
The safety of the grave is preferable
to the sneers, jeers, contempt and mockery
of this world.
My sons will be safe,
without father, without home, without refuge from danger.
And now, I admit my life's great error.
I left my father's house, seduced
by Jason's oily words. But heaven is
my friend, and Jason shall pay for his crime.
He'll never see his sons again in this life.
He'll never father a child from his fresh young
princess. She will die the death she deserves,

the death of my poison. Nobody
on this earth will call me weak.
Medea is the real strength
of woman, the strength that
for centuries has been subdued,
submerged and piously enslaved.
No, I am not weak.

I am a devoted friend,
a deadly enemy.
In its heart of hearts,
that is the kind of person
the world most admires.
I am set to win the admiration of the world –
for what it's worth!

CHORUS. I beg you not
    to commit these murders.

MEDEA. There is no other way for justice to be done.
    Murder is the instrument of justice.
    You have not suffered wrong like me.

CHORUS. It would be like cutting the heart
    out of your own breast.

MEDEA. I will murder my sons.
    That is how I can hurt my husband most.
    Hurting my husband is the purpose of my life.
    No hurt, human or inhuman, can hurt him enough.

CHORUS. This will make you the most miserable
    woman in the world.

MEDEA. Let it. From now on, words are
    useless. (*To the* NURSE.) Please
    go now and courteously request
    Jason to visit me. Whenever I
    need loyalty, it is to you
    I turn. Say nothing of what
    I intend to do; you are
    a woman and my loyal servant.
    Stay true to me: bring Jason here.

Exit NURSE.

CHORUS. Medea, do not murder your children.
You murder your own flesh and blood
but plan your own safety
in one of the most fragrant and fertile
countries under the Sun, favoured by
heaven from the beginning. These people
are children of the blessèd gods.
Love lives in the air.
                            Will you dare,
killer of your own children, to enter
and live in that land of sacred rivers
and hospitable homes? It is sacrilege
that you should even think of living there.
Think, Medea. Think of the nature
of sacrilege. Think, o think, Medea.
You are stabbing your children.
They are on their knees, they cry for mercy.
'Mother! Mother! Do not murder us.'
Think, Medea, think. You will be,
forever, Medea the murderess
of her own children. It would
have been more merciful
to kill them in the womb.
Abortion can be a kind of mercy.
But to let them look into the eyes
of people, to let them see the miracle
of the changing of the seasons,
to let them watch the birth and growth
and death of flowers, to let them
walk through gardens, to feel
the blessing of the summer rain,
the rebel outburst of Nature in the Spring,
the way people are born and live and die,
to learn to speak, to listen to
the fluent miracle of words – that is
a crime as great as the crime
of killing them now.
Where in the hardness of your heart
did you think of such a plan?
And in that horrible moment
when you kill your own children
where will you find the steel

56

to make inhuman your heart and hand?
When you look into their eyes,
Will you not go out of your mind
to know you are their murderess?
When your two sons fall at your feet
begging for mercy,
will you not go mad
when their innocent blood
stains your hands?
You bore them gladly in your womb.
Will you send them in great agony to their graves?
My heart will not believe it.
Your heart will never bear it.
You are not exacting revenge.
You are embracing madness.

Enter JASON.

JASON. What are you looking for, woman?

MEDEA. Jason, I ask forgiveness for everything I said.
After all the love you gave me, I can rely
on you to put up with my tantrums
and my fits of temper. I've been thinking
the whole situation out for myself.
Bitter bitch (that's how I saw myself),
what madness of mind and heart makes me
hate those who wish me nothing but good?
What madness made me treat as enemies
the just and royal rulers of this land,
and my husband who, in taking a princess
for a wife, ensuring brothers for his sons,
is merely doing what will benefit us all?
What is wrong with me? Why am I still
enraged when the gods pour
blessings on my head? Do I not have
gifted children of my own? Has it slipped
my mind that I am an exile
from my own land, lacking
real friends? These thoughts have
shown me how foolish I have been,
how blind to your generosity,
how selfish towards your selflessness

and how pointless are my jealousy and hate.
Now, dear Jason, I wish to thank you.
You are doing the right thing in choosing
this beautiful young wife.
I have been the greatest fool in the world.
I should have encouraged your plans,
helped you to fulfil them,
even stood by the marriage bed
and helped, as best I could, the young bride.
But I am what I am...a woman,
a mere woman. I beg forgiveness,
and admit my hideous mistakes.

But now, I have turned
my mind towards sanity and hope
and sincere co-operation. I have but
one desire – to help you build your happiness.
Your happiness is mine, as my heart is always yours.

Children, children, please
come here, please leave the house,
come out and greet your loving father
as I have done. Speak freely with
your father. Stand with
your mother in binding us all
together in family love, forgetting
all that former hate. The nightmare
is over; the light of love shines
through again. Take your father's
right hand.
        O God, what strange
sickness attacks my imagination?
My children, will you stretch out
your arms like that in eternity?
My tears are quicker now than
they have ever been. My fears
are bursting my heart, freezing
my blood. It is those sleepless
nights of rage and hate that
blind my loving eyes with tears.

CHORUS. I cry as bitterly as you. I cry
       because of the sheer waste that hate creates.

I pray that hatred vanish from the earth.
It does more harm than racking famine.

JASON. That's the kind of talk I like to hear, woman.
I can forgive what happened in the past.
it's natural enough for women to resent
men who marry other women,
especially younger women.
Women hate ageing, it makes their skin
like dry, wrinkled seaweed.
The sea rejects it and the land withers it.
It is sad and feeble to the touch.
It has no heart to live in its true element.
But you have changed your heart,
Medea, and for the better. It took
quite a while, of course, but at last
you have seen the happy light of reason.
From being a woman of vile abuse
you have become a wise woman.
And as for you, my sons, I have not
forgotten you. You are now perfectly safe.
I know that you will occupy
the most important positions
here in the city, with your brothers.
All you have to do now is grow to be men
like me, like Creon, like the great men of the city.
Your father, and his strong friends,
will see to the rest. May I see you,
rock-like and determined, in the full bloom
of your youth, annihilate my enemies.
Medea, why are you crying?

MEDEA. The children. I was just thinking about
the children. Growing up...becoming
men...

JASON. Why are you crying about the
children? There's no need for it.

MEDEA. I am their mother. A few moments
ago, when you were talking about
long life, grief swept through me,
because I thought their lives might
not turn out as brightly as you

predicted. I was briefly
haunted by the possibility of some
tragic disappointment, some knife
or poison in the heart of hope.

JASON. Be cheerful, Medea, I'll see to it
that things turn out for the best.
All we need is courage and determination.
Time, and the will to be important in this world,
will take care of the rest.

MEDEA. We women are weak creatures.
It takes very little to make us cry.

Just one thing remains to be said.
Since I must go into exile
(and now I see that is a just decision)
I pray that out two sons
are reared by your kind, commanding hand.
Please ask Creon to let
the children stay.

JASON. I shall ask him.

MEDEA. You could ask your wife
to intercede with Creon,
to let the children stay.

JASON. Creon will grant
permission, if I can
persuade my wife.

MEDEA. In this respect, I'd like to play my part.
I want to send the children with gifts to her,
gifts far more beautiful than any gifts
men make in these modern times:
a noble robe, and a head-dress of beaten gold.
Let there be no delay. Let one of my maids
bring the gifts immediately. What joy,
what boundless joy, will come into the heart
of your young bride, to have not only
a husband of your heroic stature,
but also finery which the Sun of all
the Heavens, the light of all the earth,
my own father's father, gave to his children.

MEDEA *takes the casket from the* NURSE *who has brought it and gives it to the* CHILDREN.

> Dear children, take these wedding gifts
> to the Princess, the happy bride,
> and give them to her
> with all your natural grace.
> These incomparable gifts will mean
> something very special to her:
> incomparable gifts best suit an incomparable woman.

JASON. Medea, you are as obstinate a woman now
> as when we lived together.
> Why do you give your richest gifts away?
> Do you think a palace such as mine
> is short of finery and gold?
> Hold on to these gifts, keep them, you'll need them yet,
> do not give them away. If my wife respects me,
> she will prefer me to all the wealth in the world
> I'm sure of that. Can't you see
> my wife will not be swayed by gifts:
> she will be swayed by me.

MEDEA. Please, please permit me to give your wife these gifts.
> Gifts please even the gods, and gold
> is mightier than a million words.
> In you, she has the greatest fortune of our time.
> Her existence makes the gods excited.
> Heaven trembles with admiration at this woman on earth.
> She is young, her father is a king.
> To save my children from exile,
> I would surrender my life,
> not merely give my gold.
>
> So go, my children,
> go to the palace and ask your father's
> beautiful young wife to let you stay in this city.
> (*Pause.*)
> Place the crown in her delicate hands.
> It is most important that you do exactly that.
> She must take my gifts into her own hands.
> Go as quickly as you can, there is no time
> to lose. May the gods attend
> your every step, and may you bring back

news to make your mother's heart
as happy as she could dream it to be.

Exeunt CHILDREN, TEACHER, JASON *and* NURSE.

CHORUS. Now, all the hope I had is dead.
    The children are in their graves already.
    The bride will wear her priceless head-dress.
    Death will come to her in a circlet of gold.
    Her own hands will accomplish this,
    standing in front of a mirror.
    How gracefully she'll step into the dress of death.
    Splendid robe, circlet of beaten gold –
    wedding gifts beyond her royal dreams.

    Poor girl! Poor bride! Poor, poor Princess!

    And you, poor, cocky Jason – unwitting
    bringer of death to your own children.
    Where is your royal family now?
    Where is your man's dream of happiness?
    Poor man. Poor Jason. Poor, poor seeker.
    And now, Medea, I cry for you.
    You will kill because you were betrayed.
    That is the one terrible fact
    that consumes your heart and mind,
    and makes your life a sword
    to be plunged into Jason's heart,
    a plausible man in a royal bed.
    I see all things clearly now
    and all the hope I had is dead.

Enter CHILDREN *with their* TEACHER.

TEACHER. My lady, here are your two sons,
    saved from exile. The royal bride
    graciously and gladly accepted your gifts.
    She took the gifts into her delicate, royal hands.
    Your sons have made glad, smiling peace with her.
    But what is wrong? What is the matter?
    Why are you so upset, when fortune
    smiles on you?
    Why do you turn away your face?

MEDEA. Misery of hell!

TEACHER. These words have nothing to do
with the happy words I have brought to you.

MEDEA. Misery! Misery of hell!

TEACHER. Have I made a mistake?
Have I unwittingly said evil words?
I thought my words were good.
Where have my words gone wrong?
What is my mistake?

MEDEA. Your words were...your words.
I do not blame you for your words.

TEACHER. Why are you crying

MEDEA. Because I must, old man, because I must.
The gods had a hand in this
My folly played its part as well.

TEACHER. Be hopeful, Medea. One day, your
children will bring you to your home.

MEDEA. Long before that day, I shall
bring them and others
to a different home. There are countless
kinds of home in this homeless world.

TEACHER. Many women have been
separated from their children.
We're only human and must put up
with all these troubles as patiently as we can.

MEDEA. I shall do precisely that.
I shall endure whatever happens.
Now please go inside
and prepare the usual food
for my children.

Exit TEACHER.

My children, o my children. A city is
assured for you where you will live
without me. But I face exile
in an unknown land, before I have set eyes
on your happiness, before I have
seen your brides, prepared your

63

marriage beds, and held high
the burning torches of good will.

My own self-will has
brought me to my misery. My sons,
did I rear you all for nothing?
Was it for nothing that I bore
the agony of your birth? There was a time
when I hoped you'd be near me
in my old age, and with your loving hands
prepare my body for the grave.
That dream is dead. Without you,
my children, mine will be a life of pain,
while you, in another land, will
never see your mother with your tender eyes.
                                        Why do
your eyes look into mine? Why smile
into my soul with your final smile?
What am I to do? Women, my heart
is water at the sight of my children's faces,
descended from the Sun. I cannot do it.
Goodbye to all the schemes and plans I had.
I shall take my children with me
into exile. Why should I hurt or
madden their father by *their* misfortune,
only to double my own grief?
No, I will not do it.
I shall bury my plans, not my children.

What is this? What is wrong? What has softened me?
I will not make a fool of myself
by letting my enemies strut about in
freedom? I *will* do it. I *will* go
through with it.

Come, my children.
Go into the palace.

The CHILDREN *move towards the door of the palace, stand there as*
MEDEA *speaks to the* CHORUS.

Whoever here doesn't
wish to witness my sacrifice
may simply turn away. My hand

is as determined as my heart.

My heart! Do not commit
this crime. Leave them alone,
leave them the right to live their lives
as they will. Even if they live
in a far country, the knowledge
that they are alive will bring me
joy enough. Knowledge that those
we love are alive and well brings
a special joy to the thinking heart.
No! No! By the dead in hell who
are condemned never to forget their crime,
this love cannot be. No son of mine
will take an insult from an enemy.
My sons must die.
I, who gave them birth, will kill them.
That woman will not escape.
Already, she wears the golden diadem
of poison on her head.
And in the poisoned robe
the shining bride is dying.
I have knowledge
of such matters – there are consequences.
Jason's beautiful young princess is dying at this moment.
I wish to speak to my children.
Let me hold your hands,
my sons, let me kiss your hands.

O dear hands of my sons
O dear mouths of my sons
O dear dear figures of my dreams
O open and noble faces
may you be happy forever
but not here.
Your father has stolen your happiness from you.
How sweet it is to touch you,
how soft is your skin,
how sweet is your breath,
my children, children of my womb.
Go! Go now! I cannot bear to look on you.

The CHILDREN *go inside.*

Grief and misery are my masters now.
Passion strangles all my love,
passion brings most of his unhappiness to man,
passion that gives fierce strength to my will.
It is my own loved children I must kill.

CHORUS. The fathers of children
are not as happy as the men
who have no children.
A man without children
never knows if children
are a blessing or a curse
and so he cannot miss a happiness
he never had, and therefore may
escape a life of slavish misery.
But those whose homes are full
of growing children that they love
are often eaten by anxiety and worry,
day after day, night after night.
How are they to rear them properly?
What schools shall they send them to?
How shall they speak to them?
How show authority and not appear tyrannical?
How be patient in the face of disobedience?
How reprimand a child without alienating him further?
And then, if educated, how shall children make a living?
If uneducated, what can be done for them?
How tolerate their surly silences,
their foolish babble, their
unbelievable friends with clowns' faces
and hair like the plucked feathers
of a thousand different birds?
How tolerate the garish absurdity
of growing up? And finally,
suppose the children have grown up properly,
how can the father know
if the child is good or bad,
ready to help the father in his old age
or ditch him like a toothless old dog?
Many a father knows what it means
to be driven into exile
in the land that helped him rear his family.

I know many a father in this city,
not far from where his son begets
more sons. It is ludicrous succession.
Many women are aware of this,
but keep their silence. What is the use of talking?

Enter MESSENGER.

MEDEA. It's curious
how evil makes men hurry,
shakes them from their lethargy.

MESSENGER. Go, Medea, get out of here.
Get out, by land or sea.
Get out! Get out!

MEDEA. Why?

MESSENGER. The Princess is dead.
So is her father, Creon.
Both dead by your poison, planted
in your beautiful gifts. Your gift
of poison has brought death and havoc.

MEDEA. From this moment, you are my friend and ally.
Already, I begin to know some peace of mind.

MESSENGER. Are you human? Do you know
what you have done?

MEDEA. Did she die in agony?

MESSENGER. When your children arrived with their father
at the palace, we rejoiced because we thought
your marriage troubles were over.
The servants whispered that you'd settled
your long quarrel with Jason. One servant
kissed your children's hands, another kissed
their hair. I myself, in joy, went
with the children to the women's rooms.
The Princess, who now occupies your place,
did not see the boys at first, but looked
at Jason longingly. Then, however,
resenting the children's presence, she
veiled her eyes and turned away her face.

Jason tried to calm her anger,
saying: 'Do not hate your friends.
Calm your temper and turn your
head this way. You must accept
your husband's friends as your own.
Please accept these gifts, and ask your father
not to send these boys into exile,
for my sake, for your strong husband's sake.'

Well, when she saw the gifts,
she relented, she promised all things
to her husband; and scarcely had Jason
and your sons left her
than she put on that most beautiful robe.
Carefully she placed the circlet of beaten gold
on her rich clustering hair
and began to achieve her perfection
before a mirror, smiling at her body.
Then she rose and walked across the room
on delicate white feet, so happy with her gifts.
Again and again, standing tall and stately,
she glanced at the dress falling in rustling beauty
round her feet.

There followed the most horrible sight
I have ever seen. The Princess's complexion
changed, she staggered to and fro,
she tried desperately to run, her limbs
were trembling like leaves
when the year is failing, and finally
managed to sink into her chair.
One of the oldest and most perceptive
of her attendants, believing she'd
been stricken by a fit of panic,
or some attack inspired by divine anger,
cried out her prayers to the gods
until she saw white foam furious on
her lips, the pupils of her eyes rolled up,
and every drop of blood abandoning her skin.
Immediately, a maid rushed out to Creon's palace,
another ran to Jason, to tell
the terrible news.
The house became a house of chaos.

68

Then the Princess, lying there, eyes closed,
groaned in agony, began to revive.
A double misfortune hit her then.
From the circlet of beaten gold upon her head
there flowed a pure consuming fire
while the incomparably beautiful robes,
the gifts of your innocent children,
began, with slow, efficient savagery,
to eat the Princess's immaculate white flesh.
Her body became a flame,
she leaped from her chair
and ran, shaking her head and hair
every way she could,
trying to throw the golden crown
off her burning head and hair.
But that circlet of beaten gold gripped hard.
Her most glorious hair became an insatiable fire
and the more desperately she shook her hair
the more fiercely the fire continued to burn.
Shrivelled and contorted by the agony of fire
she fell on the floor, and only her father
was able to recognise her, so charred
and melted her beautiful features.
Nobody could tell where her eyes were,
nobody discern the least sign of the beauty of her face.
She was a melting, ugly, burning thing.
The blood, mingling with fire, fell
in blazing drops from her head,
the flawless white flesh melted from her bones,
as the unseen poison consumed her, bit by bit.
This was the most fearsome thing I ever saw.
We were all afraid to touch the corpse,
appalled by poison and by fire,
by the black ruin that was once a fair princess.

But her father, ignorant
of what had happened, rushed into
the room and embraced the body.
Weeping and moaning, he kissed
his daughter's burnt form and cried:
'My child, my daughter, my poor daughter,
what god has brought this hideous

destruction on you?
Who burned the life out of
my only child?
O my daughter, let me be with you in death!'

When he had stopped crying and moaning,
he tried to stand upright
but he stuck to the dress
like ivy to the trunk of a tree
or an old wall. The struggles
of the old man were horrible to see,
so desperate, pathetic, futile, self-destroying.
Trying to free a leg, his daughter's
burnt body would stick to his,
and if he jerked violently, he ripped
his shrivelled flesh off his own bones.
At last, mercifully, he died.
Side by side they lay,
father and daughter,
King and Princess, unfleshed,
dead. Burnt bones.
Dead, Medea, dead.

There is no need for me
to speak of what's in store for you.
You know with what horrific precision
the punishment fits the crime.

The life of man is a shadow.
Those who are called philosophers
and masters of subtle reason
are most worthy of condemnation.
No living man knows lasting happiness
or even, perhaps, the meaning of it.
It is a pleasant word, though much
abused, and certainly misunderstood.
Two burnt corpses on a royal floor.
when good fortune flows this way or that
one man may have more money than another.
But happiness – I have no answer to that.

Exit MESSENGER.

CHORUS. Jason has been punished for his sin.

Innocent princess,
Jason's love is the cause of your death.

MEDEA. My friends, my sisters, mothers, wives,
     I am ready to kill my children
     and leave this land.
     I cannot delay, or my children
     will fall into murderous hands.
     Whichever way the wheel turns, my children must
     die. And if they must, *I* will kill them,
     I who gave them birth.
     Here is the sword.
     I must do it now.
     No thinking of my children,
     I have my unlived years to grieve for them,
     yes, to grieve.
     Though I shall kill them, at least I loved them.

CHORUS. O Earth and Sun, consider this accursed woman,
     stop her before she murders her children.
     Stop Medea from killing the children of light.
     Protect the house from murder, and the curse
     of the dead who don't forget.
     For you, Medea, the pains of birth meant nothing.
     Nothing do these lovely boys mean to you, Medea.
     Why let anger poison your heart?
     How can murder so easily take the place of love?
     Women who dare to love, what sort of evil
     do you create in men? What sort of evil
     do you discover in yourselves? This thing called love,
     how much of the world's evil has it created?

The CHILDREN *are heard within.*

     The cries. The cries. Listen to the cries.

Enter JASON.

JASON. You there, standing in front of this house,
     is Medea still inside? Or has she
     escaped? She had better hide in the earth
     or fly into the sky, if she wishes
     to avoid my vengeance.

CHORUS. Jason, your children are dead,
  murdered by their mother.

JASON. What?

CHORUS. Your children are dead,
  murdered by their mother,
  go see the corpses
  in their blood.

JASON. The bodies. Let me see the bodies
  (*Pause.*)
  Where is that woman? Let me kill her!

MEDEA *appears in a chariot. She has the bodies of the* CHILDREN.

MEDEA. What's all this talk of killing?
  Are you searching for the bodies and me
  who did the deed? Don't bother. If you
  have something to say to me, say it now,
  but you shall never touch me. I have
  a magic chariot, a pure, unpoisoned gift
  of the Sun, my father's father, to protect me
  against my enemies, plausible man.

JASON. You are the coldest murderess that ever lived.
  You are an evil plague that will infect the world.
  There's a demon in you, whom the gods
  have set against me. You murdered your brother.
  Then you married me with your murderous
  heart. You bore my children whom you have
  murdered because I left your bed. You
  are not a woman, you are the embodiment of hate.
  May the devil take you for his wife,
  murderess of your children, and may you populate hell
  with monsters like yourself. I shall never
  see alive the children I begot and reared and lost.

MEDEA. You are a fool,
  as King Creon was a fool to grant me one day of freedom.
  You could not hope, nor could your princess hope
  to scorn my love, the love of magical Medea.
  You are a fool, thinking to make a fool of me,
  and live happily forever after, as in some childish legend.
  You and your princess and Creon are a legend of fools.

Two fools burnt, the third fool
a whimpering, abusive, shattered parody of man.
Call me what you will, abominable, evil, poisonous.
I don't care, now that I've got
beneath your skin into your heart.
That's the special poison
I reserved for you.
My grief is nothing when I know
you cannot mock me. Your mockery is
impotent as you will be. Sorrow,
when deep enough, castrates a man.
Do you not already feel a certain weakness,
a certain helplessness? Will you be a father
ever again? Give some thought to that.
Ask yourself the simple question – what is Jason now?

JASON. I did not murder them.

MEDEA. You insulted me.

JASON. Because I scorned your love
you believed it was your right to murder?

MEDEA. You insulted me.

JASON. You are completely evil.

MEDEA. Your children are dead.

JASON. No! They live in me to bring
dread curses on your head.
(*Pause.*)
Let me bury my sons.

MEDEA. No! I shall bury my sons with my own hands,
taking them where no enemy may do violence
to their graves. In time, I shall,
through rites and rituals, expiate
their murder. I shall live with a man
of my choice. You shall die as you
deserve, now that you have seen
how death has so attended
your living marriage in a state
of gold and fire and agony.
Your promised blessing is your life's curse.

JASON. May the innocent blood of my children
        drown you in endless nightmare.

MEDEA. Only a foolish God would listen to you,
        breaker of oaths. And there are no foolish gods.
        The world is full of foolish men.
        Among such foolish men, you are the total fool.
        (*Pause.*)
        Go bury you wife.
        You know little of grief now. Wait patiently
        for your old age. Then, there's nothing
        left but memory. Some griefs deepen
        with memory, become more real
        than when they happened first.
        Do you look forward to old age?

JASON. O my children, o my dear, dear children.

MEDEA. Are you hurt, Jason? Jason, are you hurt to know
        you're not the man who won the Golden Fleece
        or planned a royal family
        but a man, a poor, sad, pointless man
        who has no wife, no home, no children?

JASON. My sons! My sons! Let me kiss their mouths.
        For god's sake, let me touch the sweet, soft
        skin of my children. Please, let me touch them.
        Once, once only. Let me touch them once.

MEDEA. No, Jason. The truth is you gambled and lost.
        You will never touch your children again.
        I killed them. That is all you know.
        I killed them. You will never touch them again.
        That is all I permit you to know.
        There's nothing left of you in me.
        How much of me is left in you?

JASON. I curse you.

MEDEA. Curse yourself.
        You never did; you never could
        and that is why no god will
        stoop to bless you.

Exit JASON.

74

CHORUS. Medea is in full possession of her own life
and of her beloved dead.
In a short time, Jason is a childless wreck.
The gods are not capricious, but they are
unpredictable. What was expected has not been
accomplished; what was unexpected has come
to happen. That is the end of the story.
And yet I wonder, and will always wonder –
Is Medea's crime Medea's glory?

ALSO FROM BLOODAXE BOOKS

The Book of Judas
A POEM BY
BRENDAN KENNELLY

In his long poem *Cromwell* (1983) Brendan Kennelly explored the complex character and motivation of a man whose name even today is uttered with automatic hatred throughout Ireland. Kennelly let Cromwell speak for himself in a poem that investigated and revealed the ferocious clichés of history, and the murderous ongoing consequences of conscious and unconscious bigotry and hatred.

Kennelly has said that 'poetry must find its voices in the byways, laneways, backyards, nooks and crannies of self'. Now, in *The Book of Judas*, an epic poem in twelve parts, Kennelly lets Judas, the eternal traitor and scapegoat, who is not merely lost but irredeemable, speak, dream and murmur in all his voices – of past and present, history and myth, good and evil, men, women and children, and moneymoneymoney – until we realise that the damned outcast, the unspeakable perpetrator of the apparently unthinkable, in penetrating the icy reaches of his own world, becomes a sly, many-voiced critic of ours.

In this poem we meet a Judas who is severed and articulate, cold and fiery, ancient and contemporary, an essential part of our culture, and of each one of us, skilled in the necessary, appalling art of judging each other.

Paperback:	ISBN 1 85224 171 3	£8.95
Hardback:	ISBN 1 85224 170 5	£25.00

Also available in a special limited signed handbound edition of 30 copies (ISBN 1 85224 172 1) for 30 pieces of silver (IR£300).

ALSO FROM BLOODAXE BOOKS

Cromwell
A POEM BY
BRENDAN KENNELLY

'This is an astonishing book...an intense poetic outcry. It is energy and honesty that make this book of horrors humanly tolerable' – SEÁN LUCY, *The Tablet*

'Brendan Kennelly has got guts. And a large portion of those are served up here. This book is not for the squeamish' – MARK PATRICK HEDERMAN, *Irish Literary Supplement*

'One of the most extraordinary books I have ever come across in my life' – GAY BYRNE, *The Late Late Show (RTE)*

'What marks Kennelly out as a writer of extreme psychological subtlety is the give in his treatment of Cromwell: an exacting judgement on the historical truth is tempered with mercy in the shape of comedy' – GILES FODEN, *Times Literary Supplement*

'These poems are shocking...he only deals, and can only deal, in strong poisons' – MARTIN DODSWORTH, *The Guardian*

'*Cromwell* is explosive, expansive, prolific, explicit' – EDNA LONGLEY

'For Kennelly, a poetic voice, like a nation, is never itself alone, and *Cromwell* provides an important and unsettling example of this difficult dependence, an openness to history that does not rely on the self as an escape-route from nightmare, or upon the integrity of the individual voice as a guarantee of poetic value' – PETER McDONALD, *Irish Review*

'Kennelly has invented a Cromwell for the modern conscience, a figure to taunt the comfortable soul of a progressive Dubliner' – PETER PORTER, *Observer*

'*Cromwell*...where all the voices that are in Brendan Kennelly are let loose to cry out against one another. That is how he thinks of poetry' – PETER LEVI, *Independent*

Paperback: ISBN 1 85224 026 1   £7.95

ALSO FROM BLOODAXE BOOKS

A Time for Voices
SELECTED POEMS 1960-1990

BRENDAN KENNELLY

'A voice and a vision...wild and unafraid – unique in contemporary poetry' - MICHAEL LONGLEY, *Irish Times*

'With *A Time for Voices*, Kennelly can be included among the Irish greats' – HAYDEN MURPHY, *Scotland on Sunday*

'With considerable honesty and bravery Kennelly enters and becomes others in order to perceive, understand and suffer...always moving, probing and doubting, never willing or able to settle on any one certainty. There is clash and conflict, cruelty and irony, sardonic wit and passion...a unique book from a poet whose range and vision is not pigeon-holed' – AIDAN MURPHY, *Sunday Press*

'Kennelly has always had the courage to write in bad taste...to move into areas that other poets seldom approach, and this selection maps a unique, and often a savage, *terra incognita*...a troubling book, exuberantly engaged, vital, and sometimes threatening; its poetry is authentic, not authoritative...Kennelly's energy remains unabated' – PETER McDONALD, *Irish Times*

'One would hate to be one of the warty lads, the fine liars, whom Yeats and the Muse prefer. All honour then to a poet who has ploughed decently and with sobriety through the Fifties and Sixties and so on, and who has attained the position of a genuine and major poet' – PETER LEVI, *Independent*

'Kennelly is a medium: he makes bread, sand, water, silence, history and people speak in their own accents...this selection from 30 years of poetry is overwhelmingly bleak...the most cheerful of our poets is also the most desolate' – AUGUSTINE MARTIN, *Irish Independent*

Hardback: ISBN 1 85224 096 2   £14.95
Paperback: ISBN 1 85224 097 0   £7.95

Also available in a special limited signed slipcased edition of 100 copies (ISBN 1 85224 081 4) at £50.

Brendan Kennelly was born in 1936 in Ballylongford, Co. Kerry, and was educated at St Ita's College, Tarbert, Co. Kerry; at Trinity College, Dublin, where he gained his BA, MA and PhD, and Leeds University. He has lectured in English Literature at Trinity College since 1963, and became its Professor of Modern Literature in 1973. He has also lectured at the University of Antwerp and in America, at Barnard College and Swarthmore College. He has won the AE Memorial Prize for Poetry and the Critics' Special Harveys Award.

He has published more than twenty books of poems, including *My Dark Fathers* (1964), *Collection One: Getting Up Early* (1966), *Good Souls to Survive* (1967), *Dream of a Black Fox* (1968), *Love Cry* (1972), *The Voices* (1973), *Shelley in Dublin* (1974), *A Kind of Trust* (1975), *Islandman* (1977), *A Small Light* (1979) and *The House That Jack Didn't Build* (1982). *The Boats Are Home* (1980) is still available from Gallery Press and *Moloney Up and At It* from the Mercier Press (Cork and Dublin).

His best-known work is the popular and controversial book-length poem-sequence *Cromwell*, published in Ireland by Beaver Row Press in 1983 and in Britain by Bloodaxe Books in 1987.

His books of poems translated from the Irish include *A Drinking Cup* (Allen Figgis, 1970) and *Mary* (Aisling Press, Dublin 1987), and his translations are now collected in *Love of Ireland: Poems from the Irish* (Mercier Press, 1989). He edited *The Penguin Book of Irish Verse* (1970; 2nd edition 1981), and has published two novels, *The Crooked Cross* (1963) and *The Florentines* (1967).

He is also a celebrated dramatist whose plays include versions of *Antigone*, produced at the Peacock Theatre, Dublin, in 1986, and *Medea*, premièred in the Dublin Theatre Festival in 1988, toured in England in 1989 by the Medea Theatre Company, broadcast by BBC Radio 3 in 1991 and published by Bloodaxe Books in 1991. His stage version of *Cromwell* played to packed houses at Dublin's Damer Hall in 1986 and 1987, and in London in 1991. His selection *Landmarks of Irish Drama* was published by Methuen in 1988.

His other books include *The Real Ireland*, a book of photographs by Liam Blake with text by Brendan Kennelly (Appletree Press, Belfast, 1984), and *Ireland Past and Present*, edited by Brendan Kennelly (Chartwell Books, New Jersey, 1985).

He has published five volumes of selected poems: *Selected Poems* (Allen Figgis, 1969), *Selected Poems* (Dutton, New York, 1971), *New and Selected Poems* (Gallery Press, 1976), *Selected Poems* (Kerrymount, Dublin, 1985), and *A Time for Voices: Selected Poems 1960-1990* (Bloodaxe Books, 1990). His epic poem *The Book of Judas* is published by Bloodaxe Books in 1991.